TO WIN

Dream to Win – Olympic Gold

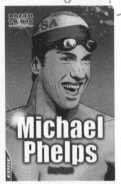

Michael Phelps

978 0 7496 9028 1 pb
978 1 4451 1417 0 eBook

Chris Hoy

978 0 7496 9196 7 pb
978 1 4451 1419 4 eBook

Rebecca Adlington

978 0 7496 9195 0 pb
978 1 4451 1418 7 eBook

Other titles in the series:

Wayne Rooney

978 0 7496 9551 4 pb
978 1 4451 1421 7 eBook

Tiger Woods

978 0 7496 9550 7 pb
978 1 4451 1420 0 eBook

David Beckham

978 0 7496 8232 3 pb
978 1 4451 1444 6 eBook

Lewis Hamilton

978 0 7496 8233 0 pb
978 1 4451 1445 3 eBook

Hope Powell

978 0 7496 8235 4 pb
978 1 4451 1415 6 eBook

Monty Panesar

978 0 7496 8234 7 pb
978 1 4451 1414 9 eBook

Andy Murray

978 0 7496 9027 4 pb
978 1 4451 1416 3 eBook

This edition 2012

First published in 2010 by
Franklin Watts
338 Euston Road
London NW1 3BH

Franklin Watts Australia
Level 17/207 Kent Street
Sydney NSW 2000

Text © Roy Apps 2010
Illustrations © Chris King 2010
Cover design by Peter Scoulding

A CIP catalogue record for this book
is available from the British Library.

ISBN: 978 0 7496 9551 4

Dewey Classification: 796.3'34'092

5

Printed in Great Britain

Franklin Watts is a division of Hachette Children's Books,
an Hachette UK company.
www.hachette.co.uk

Wayne Rooney

Roy Apps

Illustrated by Chris King

LONDON·SYDNEY

Chapter One:

Ten Year Old
Beats Top Goalie!

20th April 1996. Anfield Football Ground,
Liverpool. The stadium is packed for the
Liverpool v Everton Merseyside derby game.
Suddenly, a huge roar erupts from the crowd
as the teams run on to the pitch.

First out are the team captains and match day mascots. Today, Everton's mascot is a ten-year-old lad with cropped ginger hair and freckles.

Before the match begins the team mascot is allowed to have a few goes taking shots at the club goalkeeper. The Everton goalkeeper is Neville Southall who has played over 500 games for the club. Lots of match day mascots have fired shots at him. Some of them had hit the ball on target; others had missed the ball completely and a few had simply fallen over.

Today's mascot watches the goalkeeper come off his line, then places the ball a little way outside the penalty area and takes a couple of steps back. His shot takes the goalie completely by surprise. It's a very high chip shot; one that he's been practising. Neville Southall stretches wide to his left to try and tip the ball over the bar, but he can't quite manage it. The ball sails past his outstretched hand and lands in the back of the net. The young mascot punches the air in triumph.

The goalkeeper picks the ball out of the net. Being one of the best goalkeepers in the world, he doesn't like being beaten by a ten-year-old boy. "You're a flash young beggar, aren't you?" he tells the mascot crossly.

The mascot just shrugs. As he runs off the pitch, an announcement comes over the loudspeaker: "A big hand for today's Everton mascot, ten-year-old Wayne Rooney!"

Chapter Two:

Football Mad

Everybody in Wayne Rooney's family was
an Everton fan. So were all his friends and
everybody else on the estate in Croxteth,
Merseyside where he lived. On match days,
windows in the street would be decorated
with blue-and-white Everton scarves and flags.

Wayne had been virtually born an Everton fan. His dad was desperate to name him 'Adrian', after the famous Everton midfielder Adrian Heath. His mum had other ideas.

"Our son is not going to be named after a footballer," she said. "He's our eldest, so he'll be named Wayne, after his father and that's the end to it." When baby Wayne was six months old, he was taken by his dad to his first football match at Everton's home ground, Goodison Park. Six months after that, Wayne's dad was showing him how to kick a ball.

In the playground; on the pavement; over at the tarmac pitch behind the boys' club, Wayne and his mates spent all their spare time kicking a football around. They were football mad. Every year they had two dreams: that Everton would win the FA Cup and that their rivals Liverpool would be relegated.

All the pubs in the area had boys' football teams, and Wayne played for Copplehouse in the under-nines' league.

Parents used to come to the matches to cheer their sons on. One day after a match, Wayne saw his dad talking to a man he didn't recognise. It looked as if they were talking about something serious. Wayne saw his father shake hands with the man. Then his dad came over to him.

"Who was that, Dad?" asked Wayne.

"He's a football scout. The club he works for are interested in giving you a trial. If you do well, they'd like you to sign schoolboy forms for them."

Wayne gulped. "You mean I could soon be playing schoolboy football for Everton?"

His dad shook his head. "No, Wayne, the scout wasn't from Everton. He was from Liverpool."

Wayne couldn't believe it. He had been spotted by a scout, but the club was Liverpool, Everton's arch rivals!

Chapter Three:

Out of Place

The following week, Wayne went along to Liverpool's training ground for the trial. He quickly realised that everybody was staring at him. At first he couldn't work out why. He looked just the same as all the other nine-year-old boys there, didn't he?

Then he got it: he was wearing his Everton shirt! Every day, as soon as he came home from school, he took off his school jumper, tie and shirt and put on his blue Everton shirt. And he'd done exactly the same that afternoon.

Everyone practised their skills and then there were some five-a-side matches. Each time Wayne touched the ball, he sensed the Liverpool coaches and all the other boys glaring at him in his Everton shirt. He'd never felt so out of place in his life.

A few days later, Wayne got a letter from Liverpool inviting him to a second trial.

"Don't worry, son," said his dad, "your mum and I won't kick you out if you become a Liverpool player."

"No, but my mates and my cousins aren't going to like it," said Wayne, gloomily. He knew the old saying: 'once a Blue, always a Blue.'

One evening a few days before the second Liverpool trial, Wayne came in from playing football with his mates. His dad was in the hallway, putting the phone back.

"I've got some good news," he told Wayne. "I've just had a phone call from another football scout who saw you playing for Copplehouse at the same time as the Liverpool scout. He wants to give you a trial."

"Which club is he from?" asked Wayne.

"Everton!" his dad replied with a smile.

"Yes!" shouted Wayne.

"The only problem is," Wayne's dad went on, "that trial's on the same evening as the Liverpool trial. You can't go to both. Which one will you choose?"

"Dad," replied Wayne, with a sigh, "there's not a choice to make."

Chapter Four:

Once a Blue, Always a Blue

The Rooney family didn't have a car, so Wayne and his dad went to the Everton ground on the bus.

This time, Wayne knew he wouldn't be out of place wearing his Everton shirt. His dad sat beside him, fidgeting nervously.

"Sit still!" exclaimed Wayne. "I'm the one who should be nervous."

"But suppose I get to meet Joe Royle," said Wayne's dad. "I'm sure I wouldn't know what to say." Joe Royle was the Everton manager and one of Wayne's dad's all-time heroes.

The trial was a bit like the Liverpool one: ball skills, followed by five-a-side matches. Afterwards, Wayne sat on the touchline, waiting for his dad. How long would he have to wait before he got a letter saying whether or not Everton wanted him, he wondered? A few days; a week; a fortnight? It made him sick just thinking about it.

Suddenly, Wayne felt a hand on his shoulder. He turned round. There was his dad, with a broad grin on his face.

"Don't tell me, you met Joe Royle," Wayne asked him.

His dad shook his head. "No, something even better. I've been talking to the Youth Development Officer. They want you to sign schoolboy forms right away!"

Wayne and his dad rushed home to tell his mum the news. She burst into tears. Then he celebrated in the best way possible: by having a kick about with his mates.

Wayne joined 139 other boys at Everton's Centre of Excellence. In his first season, he played 30 games for them. They lost only once, against Liverpool, and Wayne scored a total of 114 goals, including 6 in one game against Manchester United!

Wayne played for and trained with the Centre of Excellence all the time he was at secondary school. When he reached the age of 16, he signed professional papers for Everton.

"Didn't you ever think of signing for a big club, like Man United or Liverpool?" his cousin Toni teased him one day.

"No," said Wayne. "Once a Blue, always a Blue. That's me."

"Don't believe you," said Toni. "You fancy that Coleen McLouglin, and she and her family are all big Liverpool fans. If you went out with her, you'd have to support Liverpool."

Toni was right. He did like Coleen McLouglin. He thought she was the fittest girl on the estate. He looked crossly at Toni. "Listen," he told her, "I'm Everton, through and through, me." And to prove it, he got Toni to write the words 'once a Blue, always a Blue' on his T-shirt.

And it was that T-shirt and those words that the 15,000-strong crowd saw when Wayne pulled his football shirt off after scoring the first goal for the Everton Youth Team in the 2002 FA Youth Cup Final against Aston Villa.

That goal and the T-shirt made sure that when Wayne made his first-team debut at the start of the following season, all the Everton fans knew who he was. He came on as a substitute to the sound of the home crowd chanting "Roo-nee! Roo-nee!"

Wayne was already an Everton hero, playing professional football for the club he loved. All his dreams seemed to be coming true.

Nothing could go wrong now.

Could it?

Chapter Five:

Liverpool Girl

Four days before he made his Everton debut, Wayne had been hanging about the fish and chip shop. He was having a kick about with his mates, when two girls came along on a bike; one of the girls was Wayne's cousin, Claire, the other girl was Coleen McLouglin.

Just as they passed Wayne and his mates, the chain came off the bike. Coleen got down and started trying to fix it. Wayne watched Coleen. He had been right. She was very pretty. He would've asked her out before, but for two things: one, he was too shy, and two, she was a Liverpool supporter.

He bent down and started to fix the bike chain. His mates sniggered and grinned.

It took him quite a while to fix the chain, partly because he'd never fixed a bike chain before, and partly because he was trying to decide whether he could dare ask out a girl who was a Liverpool supporter.

Eventually, he got up and said to Coleen: "There, that's fixed it. Would you like a date with me?"

"OK," Coleen replied.

So they got some chips and went for a walk round the estate.

The evening after his Everton debut, Wayne took Coleen out for a walk again. Standing on the doorstep to her house afterwards, Wayne gave Coleen a goodnight kiss.

"What's it like, kissing a girl who supports Liverpool?" Coleen asked.

"Er… all right…" replied Wayne, a little unsurely. What a daft question. It was the best thing ever!

"What's it like kissing an Everton first-team player?" Wayne asked.

"OK," replied Coleen with a smile. "Besides, you're the best young player Everton have got. My dad says you're even good enough to play for Liverpool. So you won't be an Everton player for ever, will you?"

"Of course I will!" said Wayne.

"So, once a Blue, always a Blue, is it?" asked Coleen.

Wayne nodded uncertainly. And for the first time ever, he began to wonder.

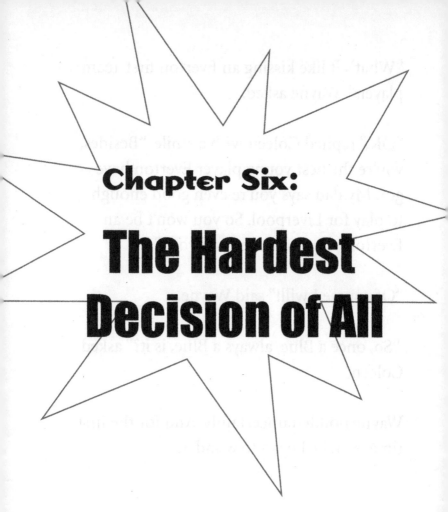

Chapter Six:

The Hardest Decision of All

Wayne's first two seasons as an Everton first-team player were great. In just his second match, he scored a last-minute winner against Arsenal to end their 30-match unbeaten run.

During this time he played for England too, scoring four goals in the 2004 European Championship Finals. Suddenly, Wayne Rooney was the hottest football player around.

But Everton were in trouble. At the end of the 2003–4 season, they had just avoided being relegated to the Championship. They were also £43 million in debt.

One evening, Wayne's agent phoned. "A top Premiership club is prepared to pay £20 million for you!" he said. "Just think of it. You'd have the chance to play Champions League football, just like your mates in the England squad."

Wayne couldn't believe it. Surely Everton wouldn't turn down that sort of money? "What's the club?" Wayne asked.

"Newcastle," replied his agent.

Good club, thought Wayne. They had finished fifth in the Premiership the previous season and had qualified to play UEFA Cup football.

Somehow though, the newspapers got hold of the story of Newcastle's offer, together with all sorts of rumours about other clubs that Wayne was meant to be about to sign for: Liverpool, Chelsea, Real Madrid…

At the next home match the Everton fans chanted Wayne's name as usual, but this time not with affection, but with anger. "Greedy Rooney, Where's your T-shirt now?" they roared. Wayne wasn't on the pitch; he'd picked up an injury playing for England, but he was very hurt by the fans' reaction.

Back home, he wondered what to do. He wanted to go to a bigger club and Everton needed the money they'd get for him to help with their debts. But did he really want to move to Newcastle?

The day before the transfer window closed, Wayne's agent called him again. "Another Premiership club has made a last-minute offer," he said. "Better than Newcastle's and it's a bigger club."

"Who?" asked Wayne.

"Manchester United," replied his agent.

"I'll think about it," said Wayne quietly.

That evening, he reached his decision: the hardest one he had ever made. He went upstairs and took out his T-shirt with the words 'once a Blue, always a Blue' on it for the last time. He carefully folded it up and put it out of sight at the bottom of the wardrobe.

Then he rang his agent. "I'm ready to talk to Manchester United," he said.

Chapter Seven:

Beginning of a Dream...

Joining a successful team like Manchester United was one thing; getting into the first team was another. Wayne still hadn't recovered from his injury.

Even when he became match fit, he still had to break into a team that was full of older and more experienced international players.

"When are you going to pick me for the first team?" Wayne asked Sir Alex Ferguson.

"When I think the time is right," the boss replied. "Just be patient."

Towards the end of September, Alex Ferguson called Wayne over to the side of the training pitch. "I want you to start against Fenerbahce," he said.

Wayne was naturally excited, but very worried, too. Was he ready? He'd not played a match for over three months. This would be his first Champions League game. He would be expected to do well. After all, he was the most expensive teenage footballer ever and the fans wanted to see what Sir Alex Ferguson had got for his money.

Would he be able to perform?

It took just 17 minutes of the match for that question to be answered. Ruud van Nistelrooy put Wayne through and he scored a brilliant goal. Ten minutes later, he got another!

When United got a penalty in the second half, Wayne grabbed the ball from Ryan Giggs.

"I'm taking this one," he said and Ryan Giggs didn't argue with him.

He placed the ball on the penalty spot. He looked at the goalie swaying on his line. He remembered the lob he'd taken to beat Neville Southall all those years ago when he'd only been a match day mascot.

He stepped back. He shot high into the top corner.

There was an almighty roar from the Old Trafford crowd.

Wayne Rooney had scored a hat trick on his Manchester United debut!

He was already a legend.

The dream had just begun…

 **Fact file**
Wayne Rooney

Full name: Wayne Mark Rooney

Born: 24 October 1985, Croxteth, Liverpool

Height: 1.78 metres

Nationality: English

1996	Aged 10, signs schoolboy terms with Everton.
2002	Scores his first League goal against Arsenal, making him the youngest ever League goalscorer at the time. BBC Young Sports Personality of the Year
2003	First England cap: at the time, the youngest ever England player, aged 17 years, 111 days; ending a record that had stood for 124 years
2003	Youngest England International scorer (Macedonia v England). Bravo Award (for the most outstanding young footballer in Europe)
2004	Top England goalscorer at Euro 2004 – 4 goals
2004	Most expensive teenage footballer in the world following transfer from Everton to Manchester United for £30 million. Hat trick for Manchester United on debut in Champions League match against Fenerbahce
2005	Professional Footballers' Association Young Player of the Year
2006	Sir Matt Busby Player of the Year
2008	England Player of the Year. FIFA Club World Cup Golden Ball Award
2009	England Player of the Year
2010-2011	Scores three goals during qualification for EURO 2012

DREAM TO WIN

Tiger Woods

"Come on, you and me are going to the swing park," Earl told his son, Eldrick. "But first of all, we've got to go to the garage. I need to put in some teeing off practice."

Eldrick picked up the toy golf club his father had given him as a present, then swung the toy club and knocked a golf ball right into the middle of the net.

"You're a natural," exclaimed Earl. "So what do you say… we go down the swing park or we stay here and play some more golf?"

In answer, Eldrick picked up his toy club and hit another ball towards the net. Eldrick's nickname was 'Tiger'.

**Continue reading this story in
DREAM TO WIN: Tiger Woods**

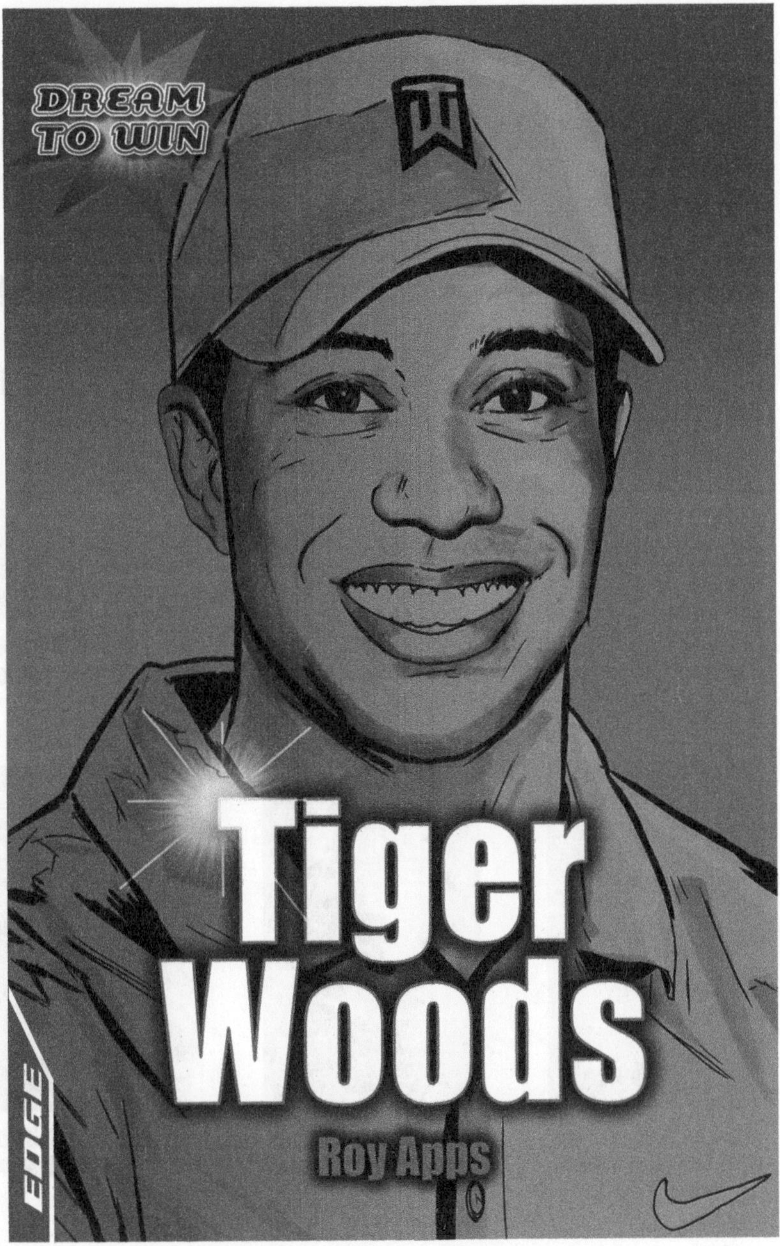
DREAM
TO WIN
Tiger
Woods
Roy Apps
EDGE

Also by Roy Apps, published by Franklin Watts:

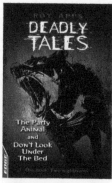

978 1 4451 0338 9 pb
978 1 4451 0853 7 eBook

978 1 4451 0336 5 pb
978 1 4451 0851 3 eBook

978 1 4451 0340 2 pb
978 1 4451 0855 1 eBook

978 1 4451 0339 6 pb
978 1 4451 0854 4 eBook

978 1 4451 0337 2 pb
978 1 4451 0852 0 eBook

978 1 4451 0341 9 pb
978 1 4451 0856 8 eBook